Pennsylvania Society

The Constitution of the Society of Sons of the Revolution

Pennsylvania Society

The Constitution of the Society of Sons of the Revolution

ISBN/EAN: 9783741124402

Manufactured in Europe, USA, Canada, Australia, Japa

Cover: Foto ©Lupo / pixelio.de

Manufactured and distributed by brebook publishing software
(www.brebook.com)

Pennsylvania Society

The Constitution of the Society of Sons of the Revolution

The Constitution

OF THE

Society of Sons of the Revolution.

AND

By-Laws and Register

OF THE

Pennsylvania Society.

INSTITUTED APRIL 3D, 1888.
INCORPORATED SEPTEMBER 29TH, 1890.

PHILADELPHIA.
1892.

OFFICERS

Pennsylvania Society.

OFFICERS

OF THE

Pennsylvania Society.

— —

President,
WILLIAM WAYNE.

Vice-President,
RICHARD McCALL CADWALADER.

Secretary,
DAVID LEWIS, Jr.
(Resigned October 10, 1892.)
ETHAN ALLEN WEAVER.

Treasurer,
SAMUEL EMLEN MEIGS.

Registrar,
JOHN WOOLF JORDAN.

Historian,
JOSIAH GRANVILLE LEACH.

Chaplain,
THE REVEREND GEORGE WOOLSEY HODGE.

Board of Managers:
JAMES EDWARD CARPENTER, *Chairman;*

WILLIAM SPOHN BAKER,	WILLIAM MACPHERSON HORNOR,
GEORGE M. CONARROE,	CHARLES HENRY JONES,
WILLIAM HENRY EGLE, M.D.,	JAMES MIFFLIN,
Rev. HORACE EDWIN HAYDEN,	Hon. SAMUEL W. PENNYPACKER.

Committee on Admissions:
JOSIAH GRANVILLE LEACH, *Chairman;*
Hon. SAM'L W. PENNYPACKER, WILLIAM MACPHERSON HORNOR.

DELEGATES

General Society.

JOHN CADWALADER,
JAMES EDWARD CARPENTER, ·
JOSIAH GRANVILLE LEACH,
HON. SAMUEL WHITAKER PENNYPACKER, LL.D.,
JOHN CLARKE SIMS.

ALTERNATES:

THOMAS HEWSON BRADFORD, M.D.,
RICHARD STRADER COLLUM, Captain U.S.M.C.,
ISAAC HIESTER,
WILLIAM CHURCHILL HOUSTON,
HON. JAMES TYNDALE MITCHELL, LL.D.

Publication Committee.

The Constitution.

T being evident, from a steady decline of a proper celebration of the National holidays of the United States of America, that popular concern in the events and men of the War of the Revolution is gradually declining, and that such lack of interest is attributable, not so much to the lapse of time and the rapidly increasing flood of immigration from foreign countries, as to the neglect, on the part of descendants of Revolutionary heroes, to perform their duty in keeping before the public mind the memory of the services of their ancestors and of the times in which they lived; therefore, the Society of the Sons of the Revolution has been instituted to perpetuate the memory of the men who, in the military, naval, and civil service of the Colonies and of the Continental Congress, by their acts or counsel, achieved the Independence of the country, and to further the proper celebration of the anniversaries of the birthday of Washington, and of prominent events connected with the War of the Revolution; to collect and secure for preservation the rolls, records, and other documents relating to that period; to inspire the members of the Society with the patriotic spirit of their forefathers; and to promote the feeling of friendship among them.

The General Society shall be divided into State Societies, which shall meet annually on the day appointed therefor in their respective by-laws, and oftener if found expedient; and at such annual meeting the reasons for the institution of the Society shall be considered, and the best measures for carrying them into effect adopted.

7

The State Societies, at each annual meeting, shall choose, by a majority of the votes present, a President, a Vice-President, a Secretary, a Registrar, a Treasurer, a Chaplain, and such other officers as may by them respectively be deemed necessary, together with a board of managers consisting of these officers and of nine other members, all of whom shall retain their respective positions until their successors are duly chosen.

Each State Society shall cause to be transmitted annually, or oftener, to the other State Societies, a circular letter calling attention to whatever may be thought worthy of observation respecting the welfare of the Society or of the general Union of the States, and giving information of the officers chosen for the year; and copies of these letters shall also be transmitted to the General Secretary, to be preserved among the records of the General Society.

The State Societies shall regulate all matters respecting their own affairs, consistent with the general good of the Society; judge of the qualification of their members or of those proposed for membership, subject, however, to the provisions of this Constitution; and expel any member who, by conduct unbecoming a gentleman or a man of honor, or by an opposition to the interests of the community in general or of the Society in particular, may render himself unworthy to continue in membership.

In order to form funds that may be respectable, each member shall contribute, upon his admission to the Society and annually thereafter, such sums as the by-laws of the respective State Societies may require; but any of such State Societies may provide for the endowment of memberships by the payment of proper sums in capitalization, which sums shall be properly invested as a permanent fund, the income only of which shall be expended.

The regular meeting of the General Society shall be held every three years, and special meetings may be held upon the order of the General President or upon the request of two of the State Societies, and such meetings shall consist of the General Officers and a representation not exceeding five deputies from each State Society, and the necessary expenses of such meeting shall be borne by the State Societies.

At the regular meeting, a General President, Vice-President, Secretary, Assistant Secretary, Treasurer, Assistant Treasurer, and Chaplain shall be chosen by a majority of the votes present, to serve until the next regular general meeting, or until their successors are duly chosen.

At each general meeting the circular letters which have been transmitted by the several State Societies shall be considered, and all measures taken which shall conduce to the general welfare of the Society.

The General Society shall have power at any meeting to admit State Societies thereto, and to entertain and determine all questions affecting the qualifications for membership in or the welfare of any State Society as may, by proper memorial, be presented by such State Society for consideration.

Any male person above the age of twenty-one years, of good character, and a descendant of one who, as a military, naval, or marine officer, soldier, sailor, or marine, in actual service, under the authority of any of the thirteen Colonies or States or of the Continental Congress, and remaining always loyal to such authority, or a descendant of one who signed the Declaration of Independence, or of one who, as a member of the Continental Congress or of the Congress of any of the Colonies or States, or as an official appointed by or under the authority of any such legislative bodies, actually assisted in the establishment of American Independence by services rendered during the War of the Revolution, becoming thereby liable to conviction of treason against the Government of Great Britain, but remaining always loyal to the authority of the Colonies or States, shall be eligible to membership in the Society.

The Secretary of each State Society shall transmit to the General Secretary a list of the members thereof, together with the names and official designations of those from whom such members derive claim to membership, and thereafter upon the admission of members in each State Society, the Secretary thereof shall transmit to the General Secretary information respecting such members similar to that herein required.

The Society shall have an insignia, which shall be a badge suspended from a ribbon by a ring of gold; the badge to be elliptical in form, with escaloped edges, one and one-quarter inches in length, and one and one-eighth inches in width; the whole surmounted by a gold eagle, with wings displayed, inverted; on the obverse side a medallion of gold in the centre, elliptical in form, bearing on its face the figure of a soldier in Continental uniform, with musket slung; beneath, the figures 1775; the medallion surrounded by thirteen raised gold stars of five points each upon a border of dark blue enamel. On the reverse side, in the centre, a medallion corresponding in form to that on the obverse, and also in gold, bearing on its face the Houdon portrait of Washington in bas-relief, encircled by the legend, "Sons of the Revolution;" beneath, the figures 1883; and upon the reverse of the eagle the number of the badge to be engraved; the medallion to be surrounded by a plain gold border, conforming in dimensions to the obverse; the ribbon shall be dark blue, ribbed and watered, edged with buff, one and one-quarter inches wide, and one and one-half inches in displayed length.

The insignia of the Society shall be worn by the members on all occasions when they assemble as such for any stated purpose or celebration, and may be worn on any occasion of ceremony; it shall be carried conspicuously on the left breast, but members who are or have been officers of the Society may wear the insignia suspended from the ribbon around the neck.

The custodian of the insignia shall be the General Secretary, who shall issue them to members of the Society under such proper rules as may be formulated by the General Society, and he shall keep a register of such issues wherein each insignia issued may be identified by the number thereof.

The seal of the Society shall be one and seven-eighths inches in diameter, and shall consist of the figure of a Minute-man in Continental uniform, standing on a ladder leading to a belfry; in his left hand he holds a musket and an olive branch, whilst his right grasps a bell-rope; above, the cracked Liberty Bell; issuing therefrom a ribbon bearing the motto of the Society, *Exegi monumentum ære perennius;* across the top of the ladder, on a ribbon, the figures 1776; and on the left of the minute-man, and also on a ribbon, the figures 1883, the year of the formation of the Society; the whole encircled by a band three-eighths of one inch wide; thereon at the top thirteen stars of five points each; at the bottom the name of the General Society, or of the State Society to which the seal belongs.

By-Laws.

SECTION I.

Members shall be elected as follows: Candidates shall send their names and documents, or other proof of qualifications for membership, to the Board of Managers, and, upon a favorable report from said Board, and upon payment of the initiation fee, may thereupon become members of the Society.

SECTION II.

The initiation fee shall be five (5) dollars; the annual dues three (3) dollars: *Provided*, That any member who shall have been elected during the last three months of the fiscal year shall not be required to pay the annual dues for the current fiscal year. The payment at one time of fifty (50) dollars shall constitute a life membership. The payment at one time of one hundred (100) dollars shall constitute a perpetual or endowed membership, and upon the death of a member so paying, the membership shall be held by his eldest son, or such other descendant from the ancestor from whom he claims as he may nominate; in failure of such nomination having been made, the Society may decide which one of the descendants shall hold the membership: *Provided always*, that the Society reserves to itself the privilege of rejecting any nomination that may not be acceptable to it. All those holding life or endowed memberships shall be exempt from the payment of the initiation fee and annual dues.

SECTION III.

All initiation, life, and endowed membership fees, as well as donations which shall hereafter be paid the Society, shall remain forever to the use of the Society, of which the interest only shall be used.

SECTION IV.

The annual meeting of the Society shall be held on the third day of April, at which a general election of officers by ballot shall take place, except when such date shall fall on Sunday, in which event the meeting shall be held on the following day. In such election a majority of the ballots given for any officer shall constitute a choice; but if, on the first ballot, no person shall receive such majority, then a further balloting shall take place, in which a plurality of votes given for any officer shall determine the choice.

SECTION V.

At all meetings of the Society ten (10) members shall constitute a quorum for the transaction of business.

SECTION VI.

The President, or in his absence the Vice-President, or in the absence of both, a chairman *pro tempore*, shall preside at all meetings of the Society, and shall have a casting vote. He shall preserve order, and shall decide all questions of order, subject to an appeal to the Society.

SECTION VII.

The Secretary shall conduct the general correspondence of the Society. He shall notify all members of their election, and of such other matters as he may be directed by the Society. He shall have charge of the seal, certificate of incorporation, by-laws, and records of the Society, and shall issue certificates of membership. He, together with the presiding officer, shall certify all acts of the Society. He shall, under the direction of the President or Vice-President, give due notice of the time and place of all meetings of the Society,

and attend the same. He shall keep fair and accurate records
of all the proceedings and orders of the Society; and shall
give notice to the several officers of all votes, orders, resolves,
and proceedings of the Society affecting them or appertaining
to their respective duties. He shall be Secretary of the
Board of Managers and shall keep the record of their meetings in the regular minute book of the Society.

SECTION VIII.

The Treasurer shall collect and keep the funds and securi-
ties of the Society; and so often as those funds shall amount
to one hundred (100) dollars, they shall be deposited in some
bank or trust company in the City of Philadelphia, .to the
credit of " The Pennsylvania Society of Sons of the Revolution," and shall be drawn thence on the check of the
Treasurer for the purposes of the Society only. Out of these
funds he shall pay such sums as may be ordered by the
Society or by the Board of Managers. He shall keep a true
account of his receipts and payments, and, at each annual
meeting, render the same to the Society, when a committee
shall be appointed to audit his accounts. He shall give such
security as shall be required by the Board of Managers.

SECTION IX.

The Registrar shall keep a roll of members, and in his
hands shall be lodged all the proofs of membership qualification, and all the historical and other papers of which the
Society may become possessed; and he, under the direction
of the Board of Managers, shall make copies of such similar
documents as the owners thereof may not be willing to leave
permanently in the keeping of the Society. He, if practicable,
shall be a member of the Historical Society of Pennsylvania.

SECTION X.

The Historian shall keep a detailed record, to be deposited
with the Secretary, of all the historical and commemorative

celebrations of the Society ; and he shall edit and prepare for publication such historical addresses, essays, papers, and other documents of an historical character, other than a Register of Members, as the Secretary may be required to publish ; and at every annual meeting, if there shall be a necrological list for the year then closing, he shall submit the same with carefully prepared biographies of the deceased members.

SECTION XI.

The Board of Managers shall consist of sixteen,—namely, the President, Vice-President, Secretary, Treasurer, Registrar, Historian, and Chaplain, *ex-officio*, and nine other members, at least three of whom shall not be residents of the City of Philadelphia, and all of whom shall be elected at the annual meeting. In case of a vacancy in any of these offices the Board may fill the same until the next annual election.

They shall judge of the qualifications of the candidates for admission to the Society, and, upon the recommendation of the Committee on Admissions, shall have power to elect the same to membership. They shall have charge of all special meetings of the Society, and shall, through the Secretary, call special meetings at any time, upon the written request of five members of the Society, and at such other times as they see fit. They shall recommend plans for promoting the objects of the Society, shall digest and prepare business, and shall authorize the disbursement and expenditure of unappropriated money in the treasury for the payment of the current expenses of the Society. They shall generally superintend the interests of the Society, and execute all such duties as may be committed to them by the Society. At each annual meeting of the Society they shall make a general report.

At all meetings of the Board of Managers five members shall constitute a quorum for the transaction of business.

SECTION XII.

The Chairman of the Board of Managers shall appoint annually three members thereof as a Committee on Admissions, whose duty it shall be to pass upon the qualificatons of applicants for admission to the Society, and report to the Board of Managers.

SECTION XIII.

Ayes and nays shall be called at any meeting of the Society upon the demand of five members.

SECTION XIV.

No alteration of the By-Laws of the Society shall be made unless such alteration shall have been proposed at a previous meeting, and shall be adopted by a majority of the members present at any meeting of the Society, five (5) days' notice thereof having been given to each member.

CHARTER

OF THE

Pennsylvania Society of Sons of the Revolution.

To the Honorable the Judges of the Court of Common Pleas, No. 4, of the County of Philadelphia :—

In compliance with the requirements of an Act of the General Assembly of the Commonwealth of Pennsylvania, entitled "An Act to provide for the Incorporation and Regulation of certain Corporations," approved the twenty-ninth day of April, A. D. 1874, and the supplements thereto, the undersigned, all of whom are citizens of Pennsylvania, having associated themselves together for the purpose of maintaining a Society to keep alive among themselves and their descendants the patriotic spirit of the men who, in military, naval, and civil service, by their acts and counsel, achieved American Independence; to collect and secure for preservation the manuscript rolls, records, and other documents relating to the War of the Revolution, and to promote social intercourse and good feeling among its members now and hereafter, and desiring that they may be incorporated according to law, do hereby certify

First. The name of the proposed corporation is the "Pennsylvania Society of Sons of the Revolution."

Second. Said corporation is formed for the purpose of maintaining a society for patriotic purposes in connection

17

with the War of American Independence, the collection and preservation of manuscripts, records, and documents relating to the War of the Revolution, and for social enjoyment and intercourse.

Third. The business of said corporation is to be transacted in the County of Philadelphia, State of Pennsylvania.

Fourth. Said corporation is to exist perpetually.

Fifth. The names and residences of the subscribers are as follows : WILLIAM WAYNE, Paoli, Chester County, Pennsylvania ; RICHARD M. CADWALADER, 1614 Locust Street, Philadelphia, Pennsylvania ; GEORGE H. BURGIN, 76 Chelten Avenue, Germantown, Philadelphia, Pennsylvania ; ROBERT P. DECHERT, 406 South Broad Street, Philadelphia, Pennsylvania ; JOHN W. JORDAN, 806 North Forty-first Street, Philadelphia, Pennsylvania ; J. EDWARD CARPENTER, 228 South Twenty-first Street, Philadelphia, Pennsylvania ; J. GRANVILLE LEACH, 2118 Spruce Street, Philadelphia.

Sixth. The number of Directors of said corporation is fixed at nine (9) and the names and residences of those chosen for the first year are : J. EDWARD CARPENTER, 228 South Twenty-first Street, Philadelphia, Penna.; OLIVER C. BOSBYSHELL, 4046 Chestnut Street, Philadelphia, Penna.; E. DUNBAR LOCKWOOD, Aldine Hotel, Philadelphia, Penna.; SAMUEL W. PENNYPACKER, 1540 North Fifteenth Street, Philadelphia, Penna.; HERMAN BURGIN, 76 Chelten Avenue, Germantown, Philadelphia, Penna.; THOMAS McKEAN, 1925 Walnut Street, Philadelphia, Pennsylvania ; CHARLES MARSHALL, Germantown, Philadelphia, Penna.; WILLIAM HENRY EGLE, Harrisburg, Penna.; CLIFFORD STANLEY SIMS, Mount Holly, New Jersey. There is also a President of the said corporation, a Vice-President, Secretary, Treasurer, Registrar, and Chaplain and Historian.

The officers chosen for the first year are : President, WILLIAM WAYNE, Paoli, Chester County, Pennsylvania ; Vice-

President, RICHARD M. CADWALADER, 1614 Locust Street, Philadelphia; Secretary, GEORGE H. BURGIN, M. D., Chelten Avenue, Germantown, Philadelphia; Treasurer, ROBERT P. DECHERT, 406 South Broad Street, Philadelphia; Registrar, JOHN W. JORDAN, 806 North Forty-first Street, Philadelphia; Chaplain, REV. GEORGE WOOLSEY HODGE, 334 South Thirteenth Street, Philadelphia; Historian, J. GRANVILLE LEACH, 2118 Spruce Street, Philadelphia.

Seventh. There is no capital stock.

WITNESS our hands and seals this Fourth day of July, A. D. 1890.

WILLIAM WAYNE,	ROBERT P. DECHERT,
RICHARD M. CADWALADER,	JOHN W. JORDAN,
GEORGE H. BURGIN,	J. E. CARPENTER,

J. GRANVILLE LEACH.

COMMONWEALTH OF PENNSYLVANIA, ⎱ *ss.:*
   COUNTY OF PHILADELPHIA, ⎰

Before me, the subscriber, Recorder of Deeds of said County, personally appeared RICHARD M. CADWALADER, GEORGE H. BURGIN, and J. EDWARD CARPENTER, three of the subscribers to the above and foregoing certificate of Incorporation of the "Pennsylvania Society of Sons of the Revolution," and in due form of law acknowledged the same to be their act and deed.

WITNESS my hand and official seal, this Twelfth day of July, 1890.

JOS. K. FLETCHER,
Deputy Recorder.

DECREE.

In the Court of Common Pleas No. 4, of Philadelphia County.

In the matter of the Incorporation of the " Pennsylvania Society of Sons of the Revolution."

And now to wit, this 29th day of Sept., A. D. 1890, the above certificate of Incorporation having been on file in the office of the Prothonotary of said Court since the twelfth day of July, A. D. 1890, and due proof of publication of notice of intended application having been presented to me, I do hereby certify that I have perused and examined said Instrument and find the same to be in proper form and within the purposes named in the first class of corporations specified in Section 2 of the Act of April 29th, 1874, and that purposes are lawful and not injurious to the community. It is therefore ordered and decreed that the said Charter be approved and it is hereby approved, and upon the recording of the said Charter and its endorsements and this order in the office of the Recorder of Deeds, in and for said County, which is now hereby ordered, the subscribers thereto and their associates shall thenceforth be a corporation for the purpose and upon the terms and under the name therein stated.

M. ARNOLD,
Judge of Court of Common Pleas, No. 4,
First Judicial District of Penna.

Recorded in the office for the recording of Deeds, etc., in and for the City and County of Philadelphia, in Charter Book No. 16, page 413, etc.

WITNESS my hand and seal of office, this Tenth day of November, A. D. 1890.

GEO. S. PIERIE,
Recorder of Deeds.

Register.

22

ELECTED.		RESIDENCE.
1889.	BAKER, WASHINGTON HOPKINS, M. D.,	Philadelphia.
1889.	BAKER, WILLIAM BOYD,	Philadelphia.
1889.	BAKER, WILLIAM SPOHN,	Philadelphia.
1892.	BALCH, EDWIN SWIFT,	Philadelphia.
1891.	BALCH, THOMAS WILLING,	Philadelphia.
1892.	BANNARD, CHARLES HEATH,	Philadelphia.
1891.	BARBER, EDWIN ATLEE,	West Chester, Penna.
1889.	BARCLAY, RICHARD DE CHARMS,	Philadelphia.
1889.	BARCLAY, SAMUEL JOSIAH,	Conshohocken, Penna.
1890.	BARNES, HARRY GILLUM,	Ardmore, Penna.
1892.	BARNES, JOHN HAMPTON,	Philadelphia.
1891.	BARTHOLOMEW, AUGUSTINE,	Jeanesville, Penna.
1891.	BARTON, JOHN WALTER,	Philadelphia.
1892.	BARTOW. HENRY BLACKWELL.	Philadelphia.
1892.	BARTOW, JOSIAH BLACKWELL,	Philadelphia.
1890.	BASHORE, HARVEY BROWN, M. D.,	West Fairview, Penna.
1892.	BEAUMONT, EUGENE BEAUHARNAIS,	
	Colonel U. S. A.,	Wilkes-Barre, Penna.
1888.	BEAVER, JAMES ADDAMS, LL. D.	Bellefonte, Penna.
1891.	BELL, EDMUND HAYES,	Philadelphia.
1890.	BELL, WILLIAM,	Mifflintown, Penna.
1891.	BELLAS, HENRY HOBART,	
	Captain U. S. A.,	Germantown, Phila.
1891.	DE BENNEVILLE, JAMES SEGUIN,	Philadelphia.
1888.	BENSON, EDWIN NORTH [Life Member],	Philadelphia.
1889.	BIDDLE, ALEXANDER [Life Member],	Philadelphia.
1889.	BIDDLE, ALEXANDER WILLIAMS, M. D.,	Chestnut Hill, Phila.
1889.	* BIDDLE, ALGERNON SYDNEY. (Died April 8, 1891.)	
1890.	BIDDLE, ARTHUR,	Philadelphia.
1890.	BIDDLE, CADWALADER,	Philadelphia.
1890.	BIDDLE, CALDWELL KEPPELE,	Philadelphia.
1889.	BIDDLE, LOUIS ALEXANDER,	Philadelphia.
1889.	BIDDLE, THOMAS, M. D.,	Philadelphia.
1890.	BIDDLE, WILLIAM FOSTER,	Philadelphia.
1892.	BIDDLE, WILLIAM LYMAN,	Philadelphia.
1890.	BISHOP. REV. GILBERT LIVINGSTON,	West Chester, Penna.
1890.	BISPHAM, GEORGE TUCKER,	Philadelphia.

23

Elected.		Residence.
1889.	Bissell, Frederick Meade,	Philadelphia.
1892.	Blight, William Sergeant.	Philadelphia.
1890.	Bliss, John Horace,	Erie, Penna.
1892.	Boardman, Walter, M. D.,	Lancaster, Penna.
1888.	Bonsall, William Martin,	Philadelphia.
1891.	Booth, George Rodney,	Bethlehem, Penna.
1890.	Borie, Beauveau,	Philadelphia.
1891.	Bosbyshell, Charles Albert,	Philadelphia.
1888.	Bosbyshell, Oliver Christian.	Philadelphia.
1891.	Bournonville, Antoine,	Philadelphia.
1889.	Bower, Robert Scott,	Philadelphia.
1890.	Bowman, Robert Severs,	Berwick, Penna.
1890.	Bradford, Charles Sydney, Jr.,	West Chester, Penna.
1889.	Bradford, Thomas Hewson, M. D.,	Philadelphia.
1892.	Bright, George Denis,	Philadelphia.
1892.	Brinley, Charles A.,	Philadelphia.
1892.	Brinton, John Hill, M. D.,	Philadelphia.
1891.	Brock, Horace,	Lebanon, Penna.
1891.	Brock, John William,	Philadelphia.
1891.	Brock, Robert Coleman Hall,	Philadelphia.
1891.	Brodhead, Albert,	Bethlehem, Penna.
1891.	Brodhead, Luke Wills,	Delaware Water Gap, Penna.
1891.	Brooke, Benjamin, M. D., Assistant Surgeon U. S. A.,	Fort Leavenworth, Kansas.
1891.	Brooke, Benjamin Franklin.	Philadelphia.
1891.	Brooke, Francis Maul,	Philadelphia.
1892.	Brooke, George,	Birdsboro, Penna.
1892.	Brooke, George, Jr.,	Birdsboro, Penna.
1891.	Brooke, Hunter,	Philadelphia.
1891.	Brooke, John Rutter, Brigadier-General U. S. A.,	Washington, D. C.
1890.	Brown, Frank Wigton,	West Chester, Penna.
1891.	Brown, George Le Roy, Captain U. S. A.,	Washington, D. C.
1892.	Brown, John Douglass, Jr.,	Philadelphia.
1891.	Brundage, Asa Randolph,	Wilkes-Barre, Penna.
1891.	Brundage, Richard Bulkeley,	Wilkes-Barre, Penna.

24

ELECTED. RESIDENCE.

1891.	BRUNER, WILLIAM WEISER,	Sunbury, Penna.
1891.	BELLUS, WILLIAM ELLISON,	Germantown, Phila.
1888.	BURGIN, GEORGE HORACE, M. D.,	Germantown, Phila.
1888.	BURGIN, HERMAN, M. D.,	Germantown, Phila.
1892.	BURTON, GEORGE,	Philadelphia.
1891.	BUTLER, EDMUND GRIFFIN,	Wilkes-Barre, Penna.
1891.	BUTLER, GEORGE HOLLENBACK,	Wilkes-Barre, Penna.
1891.	BUTLER, PIERCE,	Wilkes-Barre, Penna.
1891.	BYERS, ALFRED WEITZEL,	Meadville, Penna.
1889.	CADWALADER, CHARLES EVERT, M. D.,	Philadelphia.
1889.	CADWALADER, JOHN,	Philadelphia.
1888.	CADWALADER, RICHARD MCCALL,	Philadelphia.
1891.	CALVERT, JOHN,	Philadelphia.
1888.	CARPENTER, JAMES EDWARD,	Philadelphia.
1891.	CARPENTER, JAMES HOPKINS,	Camden, N. J.
1889.	CARPENTER, LOUIS HENRY,	
	Colonel U. S. A.,	Fort Reno, Indian Territory.
1888.	CARPENTER, THOMAS PRESTON,	Buffalo, N. Y.
1890.	CARSON, HAMPTON LAWRENCE,	Philadelphia.
1891.	CARVER, CHARLES,	Philadelphia.
1891.	CASTLE, WILLIAM HENRY,	Philadelphia.
1890.	CHANDLER, THEOPHILUS PARSONS,	Philadelphia.
1891.	CHASE, EDWARD HENRY,	Wilkes-Barre, Penna.
1892.	CLAGHORN, CLARENCE RAYMOND,	Philadelphia.
1892.	CLAGHORN, JAMES RAYMOND,	Philadelphia.
1892.	CLARKSON, SAMUEL,	Philadelphia.
1890.	CLEMENT, CHARLES MAXWELL,	Sunbury, Penna.
1890.	COLLUM, RICHARD STRADER,	
	Captain U. S. M. C.,	Philadelphia.
1892.	COMSTOCK, GEORGE STEDMAN,	Mechanicsburg, Penna.
1889.	CONARROE, GEORGE MECUM,	Philadelphia.
1891.	COOKE, MILLER HORTON,	Wilkes-Barre, Penna.
1888.	CRAIG, ISAAC,	Allegheny, Penna.
1888.	CROSBY, PEIRCE,	
	Rear Admiral U. S. N.,	Washington, D. C.
1891.	CROTHERS, STEVENSON,	Chestnut Hill, Phila.
1892.	CURTIN, WILLIAM WILSON,	Philadelphia.

25

ELECTED.		RESIDENCE.
1889.	CUTHBERT, ALLEN BROOKS,	Edgewater Park, N. J.
1889.	CUTHBERT, MAYLAND,	Edgewater Park, N. J.
1889.	CUYLER, THOMAS DE WITT,	Philadelphia.
1890.	DALE, RICHARD,	Philadelphia.
1890.	DANA, CHARLES EDMUND,	Philadelphia.
1891.	DARLING, THOMAS,	Wilkes-Barre, Penna.
1890.	DARRACH, JAMES, M. D.,	Germantown, Phila.
1891.	DARTE, ALFRED, JR.,	Wilkes-Barre, Penna.
1892.	DARTE, LUTHER CURRAN,	Kingston, Penna.
1891.	DAUGHERTY, THOMAS,	Audenried, Penna.
1891.	DAVIS, CHARLES GIBBONS,	Philadelphia.
1889.	DAVIS, CHARLES LUKENS, Captain U. S. A.,	San Diego, Cal.
1891.	* DAVIS, EDWARD MORRIS, JR. (Died December 27, 1891.)	
1891.	DAVIS, ISAAC ROBERTS,	Philadelphia.
1889.	DAVIS, WILLIAM WATTS HART,	Doylestown, Penna.
1888.	DECHERT, HENRY MARTYN,	Philadelphia.
1889.	DECHERT, HENRY TAYLOR,	Philadelphia.
1888.	DECHERT, ROBERT PORTER,	Philadelphia.
1890.	DIEHL, EDWARD CLARKE,	Philadelphia.
1890.	DILLARD, HENRY KUHL,	Philadelphia.
1891.	DORR, DALTON,	Philadelphia.
1891.	DORRANCE, BENJAMIN FORD,	Dorranceton, Penna.
1891.	* DORRANCE, CHARLES. (Died January 18, 1892.)	
1889.	DOUGHERTY, CHARLES BOWMAN,	Wilkes-Barre, Penna.
1890.	DOUGLASS, REV. BENJAMIN JOHNSON,	Philadelphia.
1892.	DUANE, JAMES MAY,	Philadelphia.
1892.	DUANE, RUSSELL,	Philadelphia.
1892.	DU BARRY, JOSEPH NAPOLEON, JR.,	Philadelphia.
1888.	DULL, CASPER,	Harrisburg, Penna.
1891.	DENTON, WILLIAM RUSH, M. D.,	Germantown, Phila.
1891.	DUTTON, WILLIAM DALLIBA,	Philadelphia.
1892.	ECKARD, REV. LEIGHTON WILSON, D. D.,	Easton, Penna.
1891.	EGBERT, JOSEPH CRAWFORD, M. D.,	Wayne, Penna.
1888.	EGLE, WILLIAM HENRY, M. D.,	Harrisburg, Penna.
1889.	ELWYN, REV. ALFRED LANGDON,	Philadelphia.
1890.	EMERY, TITUS SALTER,	Philadelphia.

ELECTED.		RESIDENCE.
1891.	ESTÈ, CHARLES,	Philadelphia.
1891.	ETTING, CHARLES EDWARD [Life Member],	Philadelphia.
1892.	ETTING. EDWARD JOHNSON,	Philadelphia.
1892.	ETTING, JOSEPH MARX,	Philadelphia.
1891.	ETTING, THEODORE MINIS,	Philadelphia.
1889.	EVANS, FRANK BROOKE,	Philadelphia.
1891.	EVANS, MORDECAI DAWSON,	Philadelphia.
1891.	EVANS, POWELL,	Philadelphia.
1890.	EVANS, SAMUEL,	Columbia, Penna.
1890.	EVANS, WILLIAM DARLINGTON,	West Chester, Penna.
1891.	EVERETT, HENRY LAWRENCE,	Philadelphia.
1891.	EYERMAN, JOHN,	Easton, Penna.
1891.	EYRE, WILSON, JR.,	Philadelphia.
1888.	FAGAN, MAURICE EDWARD,	Philadelphia.
1892.	FILSON, JOHN BAILY,	Germantown, Phila.
1891.	FISHER, JAMES HENRY,	Scranton, Penna.
1889.	FISHER, WILLIAM READ,	Philadelphia.
1892.	FLICKWIR, JOSEPH WILLIAMSON,	Philadelphia.
1891.	FORBES, WILLIAM INNES,	Philadelphia.
1889.	* FOX, DANIEL MILLER. (Died March 20, 1890.)	
1889.	FOX, HENRY KORN,	Philadelphia.
1889.	FOX, WILLIAM HENRY,	Philadelphia.
1890.	FRALEY, JOSEPH CRESSON,	Philadelphia.
1890.	FRAZER, JAMES PATRIOT WILSON,	Philadelphia.
1888.	FRAZER, PERSIFOR, (D. Sc. Un. de France) [Life Member],	
		Philadelphia.
1888.	GILLESPIE, GEORGE CUTHBERT,	Philadelphia.
1890.	GLENTWORTH, CHARLES EUGENE,	Norwood, Penna.
1890.	GLENTWORTH, JAMES,	Philadelphia.
1889.	GOBIN, JOHN PETER SHINDEL,	Lebanon, Penna.
1891.	GODFREY, LINCOLN,	Merion, Penna.
1891.	GREEN, EDGAR MOORE, M. D.,	Easton, Penna.
1891.	GREEN, TRAILL, M. D., LL. D.,	Easton, Penna.
1891.	GREENOUGH, EBENEZER WILLIAM,	Sunbury, Penna.
1891.	GRIFFITH, MANUEL EYRE,	Philadelphia.
1891.	GRIFFITH, ROBERT EGLESFELD,	Philadelphia.
1891.	GROSS, EDWARD ZIEGLER,	Harrisburg, Penna.

ELECTED.		RESIDENCE.
1892.	GUILLOU, VICTOR,	Philadelphia.
1890.	GUMBES, CHARLES WETHERILL, M. D.,	Oaks, Penna.
1892.	HAGER, CHRISTOPHER,	Lancaster, Penna.
1891.	HAKES, HARRY, M. D.,	Wilkes-Barre, Penna.
1892.	HALE, JOHN MILLS,	Philipsburg, Penna.
1892.	HAMILTON, HUGH, M. D.,	Harrisburg, Penna.
1892.	HAND, HENRY JESSOP,	Wayne, Penna.
1892.	HANDY, CHARLES,	Philadelphia.
1891.	HARDING, GARRICK MALLERY,	Wilkes-Barre, Penna.
1891.	HARDING, JOHN SLOSSON,	Wilkes-Barre, Penna.
1892.	HARTRANFT, LINN,	Philadelphia.
1891.	HARTRANFT, SAMUEL SEBRING,	Norristown, Penna.
1891.	HARVEY, RICHARD WISTAR [Life Member],	Philadelphia.
1891.	HAVERSTICK, GEORGE HENRY,	Philadelphia.
1890.	HAYDEN, REV. HORACE EDWIN,	Wilkes-Barre, Penna.
1891.	HAYDEN, MOZART WILLIAM,	Baltimore, Md.
1889.	HAZLEHURST, EDWARD,	Philadelphia.
1889.	HAZLEHURST, FRANCIS,	Baltimore, Md.
1891.	HEBERTON, CRAIG,	Philadelphia.
1892.	HEBERTON, GEORGE,	Philadelphia.
1891.	HEILMAN, SAMUEL PHILIP, M. D.,	Heilmandale, Penna.
1891.	HEMPHILL, ROBERT COLEMAN,	West Chester, Penna.
1891.	HENDERSON, WILLIAM HENRY, JR.,	Philadelphia.
1889.	HENDRY, PAUL AUGUSTINE,	Philadelphia.
1890.	HERMAN, JOHN ARMSTRONG,	Harrisburg, Penna.
1889.	HESS, ABRAM,	Lebanon, Penna.
1890.	HEWES, WILLIAM AUGUSTUS [Life Member],	Pottsville, Penna.
1890.	HEWSON, ADDINELL, M. D.,	Philadelphia.
1889.	HIESTER, ISAAC,	Reading, Penna.
1891.	HILLARD, LORD BUTLER,	Wilkes-Barre, Penna.
1891.	HOBART, DAVID McKNIGHT,	Philadelphia.
1890.	HODGE, CHARLES,	Philadelphia.
1891.	HODGE, REV. FRANCIS BLANCHARD, D. D.,	Wilkes-Barre, Penna.
1890.	HODGE, REV. GEORGE WOOLSEY,	Philadelphia.
1890.	HODGE, HUGH BAYARD,	Philadelphia.
1889.	HODGE, JAMES MONROE,	Philadelphia

ELECTED.		RESIDENCE.
1890.	Hodge, Thomas Leiper Janeway,	Philadelphia.
1890.	Holmes, Robert John,	Harrisburg, Penna.
1890.	Hooton, Francis Carpenter,	West Chester, Penna.
1888.	Hornor, William Macpherson,	Bryn Mawr, Penna.
1891.	Hough, Oliver,	Philadelphia.
1890.	Houston, William Churchill,	Philadelphia.
1888.	Houston, William Churchill, Jr.,	Germantown, Phila.
1890.	Howell, Joshua Ladd,	Philadelphia.
1892.	Hoyt, Henry Martyn, Jr.,	Philadelphia.
1892.	Hubbell, Frederick Brooks,	Philadelphia.
1890.	Hughes, Henry Douglas,	Philadelphia.
1890.	Hunt, William, M. D.,	Philadelphia.
1889.	Hutchinson, Charles Hare,	Philadelphia.
1891.	Hutchinson, Pemberton Sydney,	Philadelphia.
1891.	Ingham, Ellery Percy,	Philadelphia.
1892.	Ingham, William Henry,	Philadelphia.
1889.	*Jackson, Lewis Bush. (Died August 20, 1892.)	
1888.	*James, Clarence Gray. (Died March 13, 1892.)	
1890.	Janeway, Price Wetherill,	Media, Penna.
1889.	Jones, Charles Henry,	Philadelphia.
1891.	Jones, Edwin Horn,	Wilkes-Barre, Penna.
1889.	Jones, Richmond Legh,	Reading, Penna.
1888.	Jordan, John Woolf [Life Member],	Philadelphia.
1891.	Judson, Charles Francis,	Philadelphia.
1891.	Judson, Oliver Albert, M. D.,	Philadelphia.
1891.	Judson, Oliver Boyce,	Philadelphia.
1891.	Keasbey, Henry Griffith,	Ambler, Penna.
1888.	Keen, Gregory Bernard,	Philadelphia.
1890.	Keese, Francis Suydam,	Philadelphia.
1892.	Keim, Beverley Randolph,	Philadelphia.
1890.	Keim, George de Benneville,	Philadelphia.
1890.	Keim, Henry May,	Cleveland, Ohio.
1891.	Kelly, Henry Kuhl,	Philadelphia.
1892.	Kerlin, John Ware Sharpless,	Elwyn, Penna.
1889.	Keyser, Peter Dirck, M. D.,	Philadelphia.
1890.	King, William Clarence,	Williamsport, Penna.
1891.	Kirkpatrick, William Sebring,	Easton, Penna.

ELECTED.		RESIDENCE.
1892.	KNIGHT, FRANKLIN,	Philadelphia.
1892.	KOONS, SAMUEL BISPHAM,	Philadelphia.
1890.	KRUMBHAAR, ALEXANDER,	Philadelphia.
1891.	KULP, HARRY EUGENE,	Wilkes-Barre, Penna.
1891.	KULP, JOHN STEWART, M. D.,	Wilkes-Barre, Penna.
1892.	KUNKEL, PAUL AUGUSTINE,	Harrisburg, Penna.
1892.	LAMMOT, DANIEL, JR.,	Philadelphia.
1891.	LANDRETH, BURNET, JR.,	Bristol, Penna.
1892.	LANDRETH, LUCIUS SCOTT,	Philadelphia.
1892.	LANDRETH, OLIVER,	Philadelphia.
1892.	LANDRETH, WILLIAM LINTON,	Philadelphia.
1890.	LANSDALE, WILLIAM MOYLAN,	Philadelphia.
1892.	LARDNER, JAMES LAWRENCE,	Philadelphia.
1889.	LEACH, FRANK WILLING,	Philadelphia.
1890.	LEACH, JOSEPH GRANVILLE,	Philadelphia.
1888.	LEACH, JOSIAH GRANVILLE,	Philadelphia.
1890.	LEAMING, THOMAS,	Philadelphia.
1890.	LEE, BENJAMIN, M. D.,	Philadelphia.
1891.	LEE, CHARLES WILLIAM,	Wilkes-Barre, Penna.
1890.	LEE, EDWARD CLINTON,	Philadelphia.
1891.	LEE, WILLIAM JENKS,	Philadelphia.
1890.	LEIDY, JOSEPH, JR., M. D.,	Philadelphia.
1890.	* LEIDY, PHILIP, M. D. (Died April 29, 1891.)	
1892.	LEVIS, SAMUEL W.,	Philadelphia.
1888.	LEWIS, ALBERT NELSON [Life Member],	Philadelphia.
1891.	LEWIS, DAVID, JR.,	Philadelphia.
1890.	LEWIS, GEORGE MORTIMER,	Wilkes-Barre, Penna.
1891.	LINDERMAN, GARRETT BRODHEAD,	South Bethlehem, Penna.
1890.	LINDERMAN, HENRY RICHARD,	Easton, Penna.
1891.	LISLE, ROBERT PATTON,	
	Paymaster, U. S. N.,	Philadelphia.
1891.	LITTELL, CHARLES WILLING,	Philadelphia.
1892.	LITTLE, ARTHUR WILLIAMSON,	Philadelphia.
1892.	LITTLE, THOMAS,	Philadelphia.
1890.	LIVINGSTON, JOHN HENRY,	Clermont, N. Y.
1889.	LLOYD, HOWARD WILLIAMS,	Germantown, Phila.
1892.	LLOYD, ISAAC.	Philadelphia.

ELECTED.		RESIDENCE.
1888.	* LOCKWOOD, ELON DUNBAR. (Died December 31, 1891.)	
1891.	McCLINTOCK, ANDREW HAMILTON,	Wilkes-Barre, Penna.
1890.	McCONNELL, REV. SAMUEL D., D.D.,	Philadelphia.
1890.	McKEAN, HENRY PRATT, JR.,	Germantown, Phila.
1889.	McKEAN, THOMAS,	Philadelphia.
1890.	McNAIR, THOMAS SPEER,	Hazleton, Penna.
1891.	MADEIRA, HENRY,	Philadelphia.
1891.	MADEIRA, LOUIS CEPHAS,	Philadelphia.
1891.	MADEIRA, LOUIS CHILDS,	Philadelphia.
1891.	MADEIRA, PERCY CHILDS,	Philadelphia.
1891.	MANN, WILLIAM BENSON,	Philadelphia.
1892.	MARBLE, JOHN MINER CAREY,	Los Angeles, Cal.
1891.	MARCH, FRANCIS ANDREW, JR.,	Easton, Penna.
1888.	MARSHALL, CHARLES,	Germantown, Phila.
1890.	* MARSHALL, FRANCIS RIDGWAY. (Died May 14, 1892.)	
1890.	MARSTON, JOHN,	Philadelphia.
1888.	MARTIN, JOHN HILL,	Philadelphia.
1890.	MARTIN, JOHN SELBY,	Philadelphia.
1892.	MARTIN, JONATHAN WILLIS,	Philadelphia.
1892.	MASON, JOHN HAZLEHURST,	Philadelphia.
1891.	MEIGS, ARTHUR VINCENT, M. D.,	Philadelphia.
1890.	MEIGS, SAMUEL EMLEN,	Philadelphia.
1890.	MEIGS, WILLIAM MONTGOMERY, M. D. [Life Member],	
		Philadelphia.
1889.	MERCUR, JAMES WATTS,	Wallingford, Penna.
1889.	MERCUR, JOHN DAVIS, M. D.	Towanda, Penna.
1889.	MERCUR, RODNEY AUGUSTUS,	Towanda, Penna.
1891.	MERRILL, JOHN HOUSTON,	Philadelphia.
1891.	MERRILL, LEWIS,	
	Brigadier-General U. S. A.,	Philadelphia.
1891.	MESSLER, THOMAS DOREMUS,	Pittsburgh, Penna.
1891.	MIFFLIN, GEORGE BROWN,	Wayne, Penna.
1891.	MIFFLIN, JAMES.	Philadelphia.
1890.	MILLER, ELIHU SPENCER,	Philadelphia.
1890.	MILLER, HOBART,	Philadelphia.
1892.	MINER, ASHER,	Wilkes-Barre, Penna.
1891.	MINER, CHARLES ABBOTT,	Wilkes-Barre, Penna.

31

Elected.		Residence.
1890.	Mitchell, Hon. James Tyndale, LL. D.,	Philadelphia.
1891.	Mitchell, John Nicholas, M. D.,	Philadelphia.
1891.	Montgomery, Archibald Roger,	Bryn Mawr, Penna.
1891.	Montgomery, Richard Alan.	Bryn Mawr, Penna.
1890.	Montgomery, Thomas Harrison,	West Chester, Penna.
1890.	Moody, Nicholas Harris,	Philadelphia.
1891.	Moore, James W., M. D.,	Easton, Penna.
1889.	Morgan, John Buck,	Germantown, Phila.
1889.	Morris, Effingham Buckley,	Philadelphia.
1892.	Morris, Frederick Wistar,	Philadelphia.
1891.	Morris, Galloway Cheston.	Germantown, Phila.
1889.	Morris, Henry, M. D.,	Philadelphia.
1890.	Morris, Israel Wistar,	Philadelphia.
1892.	Morris, Jacob Giles,	Philadelphia.
1891.	Muhlenberg, Francis Benjamin,	Philadelphia.
1891.	Muhlenberg, Frank Peter.	Galesburg, Mich.
1892.	Neff, Jonathan Cilley,	Philadelphia.
1889.	Neilson, Lewis,	Philadelphia.
1889.	Neilson, William Delaware.	Philadelphia.
1889.	Newhall, Daniel Smith,	Philadelphia.
1891.	Newhall, Frederic Cushman,	New York City.
1890.	Nichols, Carroll Brewster,	Philadelphia.
1889.	Nichols, Henry Kuhl,	Philadelphia.
1889.	Norris, Charles Cotesworth Pinckney,	Philadelphia.
1892.	North, Clarence,	Philadelphia.
1891.	North, George Belford,	Wilkes-Barre, Penna.
1888.	North, George Humphries [Life Member],	Philadelphia.
1891.	North, Thomas Clemson,	Wilkes-Barre, Penna.
1891.	North, William Frederick,	Philadelphia.
1889.	Norton, Claude Richard, M. D.,	Philadelphia.
1889.	O'Neill, James Wilks, M. D.,	Philadelphia.
1892.	Orbison, Robert Allison,	Harrisburg, Penna.
1889.	Osborn, Benjamin Brown,	Germantown, Phila.
1890.	Osborn, John Annin,	Philadelphia.
1891.	Osbourn, Thomas Rehrer,	Philadelphia.
1892.	Packard, John Hooker, M. D.,	Philadelphia.
1891.	Parrish, Charles,	Wilkes-Barre, Penna.

ELECTED.		RESIDENCE.
1889.	PARRY, RICHARD RANDOLPH [Endowed Membership],	
		New Hope, Penna.
1891.	PARSONS, WINFIELD SCOTT,	Wilkes-Barre, Penna.
1890.	PARTHEMORE, E. WINFIELD SCOTT,	Harrisburg, Penna.
1891.	PARVIN, THEOPHILUS, M. D., LL.D.,	Philadelphia.
1889.	PATTERSON, CHRISTOPHER STUART,	Chestnut Hill, Phila.
1892.	PATTON, WILLIAM AUGUSTUS,	Radnor, Penna.
1892.	PAUL, LAWRENCE T.,	Villa Nova, Penna.
1890.	*PAULSON, CHARLES HENRY, JR. (Died September 26, 1891.)	
1891.	PAXTON, REV. JOHN R., D.D.,	New York City.
1892.	PEALE, WASHINGTON JAMES,	Philadelphia.
1888.	PENNYPACKER, HON. SAMUEL WHITAKER, LL.D. Philadelphia.	
1891.	PEPPER, GEORGE WHARTON,	Philadelphia.
1889.	PERKINS, EDWARD LANG,	Philadelphia.
1890.	PEROT, EFFINGHAM,	Philadelphia.
1890.	PEROT, ELLISTON,	Philadelphia.
1892.	PEROT, JOSEPH SANSOM.	Germantown, Phila.
1889.	PEROT, THOMAS MORRIS,	Philadelphia.
1891.	PHELPS, FRANCIS ALEXANDER,	Wilkes-Barre, Penna.
1891.	* PHELPS, JOHN CASE. (Died July 14, 1892.)	
1891.	PHELPS, WILLIAM GEORGE,	Binghamton, N. Y.
1892.	PHILLIPS, MARSHALL ALOYSIUS,	Rosemont, Penna.
1891.	PINKERTON, JOHN JAMES,	West Chester, Penna.
1891.	PINKERTON, SAMUEL STANHOPE SMITH,	Pittsburgh, Penna.
1890.	PLATT, FRANKLIN,	Philadelphia.
1890.	POLK, RUFUS KING,	Danville, Penna.
1891.	PORTER, JAMES MADISON,	Easton, Penna.
1888.	PORTER, JOHN BIDDLE,	Philadelphia.
1889.	POTTER, THOMAS JR.,	Chestnut Hill, Phila.
1889.	POTTER, WILLIAM,	Chestnut Hill, Phila.
1891.	POTTER, WILLIAM FRANKLIN,	Germantown, Phila.
1891.	POTTS, CHARLES WILLIAM.	Philadelphia.
1889.	POTTS, WILLIAM JOHN,	Camden, N. J.
1892.	POWELL, FRANCIS WHITING.	Philadelphia.
1891.	POWELL, WASHINGTON BLEDDYN,	Philadelphia.
1892.	PRIME, FREDERICK.	Philadelphia.
1889.	QUAY, HON. MATTHEW STANLEY,	Beaver, Penna.

ELECTED.		RESIDENCE.
1892.	RAWLE, FRANCIS,	Philadelphia.
1888.	RAWLE, WILLIAM BROOKE,	Philadelphia.
1889.	REA, SAMUEL,	Bryn Mawr, Penna.
1890.	READ, JOHN JOSEPH, Commander U. S. N.,	Mount Holly, N. J.
1891.	READ, JOHN RUE,	Philadelphia.
1892.	REATH, THOMAS,	Philadelphia.
1889.	REED, HON. HENRY,	Philadelphia.
1891.	RHODES, JAMES MAURAN,	Philadelphia.
1890.	RICHARDS, HENRY MELCHIOR MUHLENBERG,	Reading, Penna.
1892.	ROBERTS, GEORGE BROOKE,	Philadelphia.
1890.	ROBINS, ROBERT PATTERSON, M. D.,	Philadelphia.
1892.	ROBINSON, ANTHONY WAYNE,	Philadelphia.
1892.	ROBINSON, CHARLES NORRIS,	Germantown, Phila.
1890.	ROBINSON, ROBERTS COLES,	Germantown, Phila.
1892.	ROBINSON, THOMAS ADAMS,	Philadelphia.
1892.	ROBINSON, WILLIAM THOMAS,	Villa Nova, Penna.
1892.	ROCKAFELLOW, FERDINAND VAN DEVERE,	Wilkes-Barre, Penna.
1892.	ROWLAND, EDWARD K.,	Philadelphia.
1892.	RUSH, BENJAMIN,	Philadelphia.
1891.	RUSSELL, ALEXANDER WILSON, Pay Director U. S. N.,	Philadelphia.
1891.	RUSSELL, ALEXANDER WILSON, JR.,	Philadelphia.
1891.	RUSSELL, BENJAMIN REEVES, Captain U. S. M. C.,	Philadelphia.
1892.	RUSSELL, SLATER BROWN,	West Chester, Penna.
1892.	SAWTELLE, CHARLES GREENE, Brigadier-General U. S. A.,	Philadelphia.
1892.	SAWTELLE, EDMUND MUNROE,	South Bethlehem, Penna.
1891.	SAYRES, EDWARD STALKER,	Philadelphia.
1891.	SAYRES, HARRY,	Philadelphia.
1891.	SCOTT, ALEXANDER HARVEY [Life Member],	Philadelphia.
1889.	SCOTT, JOHN MORIN [Life Member],	Philadelphia.
1889.	SCOTT, LEWIS ALLAIRE [Life Member],	Philadelphia.
1891.	SCOTT, LEWIS ALLAIRE, JR., [Life Member],	Philadelphia.
1892.	SELLERS, COLEMAN.	Philadelphia.
1889.	SELLERS, DAVID WAMPOLE,	Philadelphia.

ELECTED.		RESIDENCE.
1888.	SELLERS, EDWIN JAQUETT,	Philadelphia.
1892.	SELLERS, HORACE WELLS,	Philadelphia.
1891.	SHARPE, RICHARD, JR.,	Wilkes-Barre, Penna.
1891.	SHEPPARD, FRANK LITTLE,	Altoona, Penna.
1890.	SHERMAN, CHARLES POMEROY,	Philadelphia.
1892.	SHERRERD, JAMES HOLLENBACK,	Philadelphia.
1892.	SHIPPEN, EDWARD,	Philadelphia.
1891.	SHOEMAKER, LAZARUS DENISON,	Wilkes-Barre, Penna.
1892.	SHOEMAKER, LEVI IVES, M. D.,	Wilkes-Barre, Penna.
1888.	SIMS, CLIFFORD STANLEY,	Mount Holly, N. J.
1889.	SIMS, JOHN CLARKE,	Chestnut Hill, Phila.
1892.	SINNICKSON, CHARLES PERRY,	Philadelphia.
1890.	SMITH, ARTHUR DONALDSON, M. D.,	Philadelphia.
1892.	SMITH, EDMUND,	Philadelphia.
1890.	SMITH, HENRY CAVALIER,	Torresdale, Penna.
1890.	SMITH, JESSE EVANS [Endowed Membership],	Torresdale, Penna.
1889.	SMITH, ROBERT WILLIAM,	Philadelphia.
1890.	SMITH, WILLIAM FARRAR,	
	Major-General, U. S. A.,	Philadelphia.
1892.	SMITH, WILLIAM POULTNEY,	Philadelphia.
1891.	SMITH, WILLIAM RUDOLPH,	Philadelphia.
1891.	SNIVELY, REV. SUMMERFIELD EMORY, M. D.,	Philadelphia.
1889.	SNOWDEN, HON. ARCHIBALD LOUDON,	
	United States Minister to Spain.	
1889.	SNOWDEN, GEORGE RANDOLPH,	Philadelphia.
1891.	SNYDER, ROBERT MORRIS,	Wilkes-Barre, Penna.
1891.	SOUDER, EDMUND ALPHONSO,	Philadelphia.
1890.	SPARHAWK, CHARLES WURTS,	Philadelphia.
1890.	SPARHAWK, JOHN, JR.,	Philadelphia.
1892.	SPARHAWK, RICHARD DALE,	Philadelphia.
1889.	SPENCER, JOHN THOMPSON,	Philadelphia.
1888.	SPROAT, HARRIS ELRIC,	Westtown, Penna.
1891.	STAPLES, CHARLES BOONE,	Stroudsburg, Penna.
1891.	STARR, ISAAC, JR.,	Philadelphia.
1891.	STEARNS, IRVING ARIEL,	Wilkes-Barre, Penna.
1891.	STEINMETZ, JOSEPH ALLISON,	Philadelphia.
1892.	STENGER, WILLIAM SHEARER,	Philadelphia.

ELECTED.		RESIDENCE.
1891.	STEVENS, REV. CHARLES ELLIS, LL. D.,	Philadelphia.
1890.	*STICHTER, THOMAS DIEHL. (Died July 24, 1892.)	
1891.	STŒVER, WILLIAM CASPAR.	Philadelphia.
1892.	STUBBS, THEODORE KIRK,	Oxford, Penna.
1889.	STULL, ADAM ARBUCKLE,	Philadelphia.
1891.	STURDEVANT, EDWARD WARREN,	Wilkes-Barre, Penna.
1891.	STURDEVANT, WILLIAM HENRY,	Wilkes-Barre, Penna.
1891.	TERRY, HENRY CLAY,	Philadelphia.
1890.	TEVIS, JOSHUA,	Philadelphia.
1889.	THOMAS, WALTER CUTHBERT,	Philadelphia.
1892.	TOBEY, ARTHUR WADDINGTON,	Philadelphia.
1891.	TUBBS, CHARLES,	Osceola, Penna.
1890.	TURNER, CHARLES PEASLEE, M. D.,	Philadelphia.
1889.	TURNER, JAMES VARNUM PETER,	Philadelphia.
1892.	TYLER, SIDNEY FREDERICK,	Philadelphia.
1892.	VANCE, CHARLES THOMPSON,	Chester, Penna.
1889.	VANUXEM, LOUIS CLARK,	Philadelphia.
1891.	VINTON, CHARLES HARROD, M. D.,	Philadelphia.
1888.	VOGELS, EDWARD PAGE,	Philadelphia.
1891.	WAINWRIGHT, CHANDLER PRICE,	Philadelphia.
1891.	WALBRIDGE, THOMAS CHESTER,	Germantown, Phila.
1890.	WALLACE, HERBERT FAIRFAX,	Philadelphia.
1891.	WALLACE, WILLIAM STEWART,	Philadelphia.
1892.	WALSH, REV. GEORGE HERBERT, D. D.,	Philadelphia.
1891.	WALSH, STEVENSON HOCKLEY,	Philadelphia.
1891.	WARREN, LUCIUS HENRY,	Philadelphia.
1889.	WASHINGTON, GEORGE STEPTOE,	Philadelphia.
1890.	*WATKINS, SAMUEL POTE, JR. (Died September 23, 1892.)	
1891.	WATTS, WILLIAM MEREDITH,	Philadelphia.
1888.	WAYNE, WILLIAM,	Paoli, Penna.
1889.	WAYNE, WILLIAM, JR.,	Rydal, Penna.
1889.	WEAVER, ETHAN ALLEN,	Philadelphia.
1888.	WEIDMAN, GRANT,	Lebanon, Penna.
1891.	WEITZEL, EBEN BOYD,	Scranton, Penna.
1891.	WEITZEL, PAUL ELMER,	Oak Lane, Phila.
1890.	WEITZEL, PAUL ROSS,	Scranton, Penna.
1891.	WETHERILL, ALBERT LAWRENCE,	Philadelphia.

36

ELECTED.		RESIDENCE.
1890.	WETHERILL, SAMUEL,	Philadelphia.
1891.	WHARTON, HENRY REDWOOD, M. D.,	Philadelphia.
1892.	WHEELER, JOHN HOWELL,	Philadelphia.
1891.	WHELEN, HENRY,	Bryn Mawr, Penna.
1890.	WHELEN, HENRY, JR.,	Philadelphia.
1889.	WHITE, FLOYD HALL,	Philadelphia.
1891.	WHITE, HUGH LAWRENCE.	Williamsport, Penna.
1890.	WHITNEY, FRANCIS NICHOLS,	Pottsville, Penna.
1892.	WILCOX, MONTGOMERY,	Philadelphia.
1892.	WILCOX, SAMUEL,	Philadelphia.
1891.	WILHELM, WILLIAM HERMAN,	
	Lieutenant U. S. A.,	Fort Stanton, N. M.
1890.	WILLIAMS, CHARLES DUANE,	Conyngham, Penna.
1890.	WILLIAMS, RICHARD NORRIS,	Conyngham, Penna.
1892.	WILSON, ALAN DICKSON,	Philadelphia.
1890.	WILSON, REV. CALVIN DILL,	Churchville, Md.
1890.	WILSON, REV. MAURICE EMERY, D. D.,	Dayton, Ohio.
1889.	WOOD, EDWARD RANDOLPH,	Philadelphia.
1891.	WOODWARD, GEORGE STANLEY. M. D.,	Wilkes-Barre, Penna.
1891.	WRIGHT, GEORGE RIDDLE,	Wilkes-Barre, Penna.
1890.	WRIGHT, JACOB RIDGWAY,	Wilkes-Barre, Penna.
1892.	ZELL, THOMAS BURD,	Danville, Penna.
1891.	ZIEGLER, JAMES PATTERSON, M. D.,	Mount Joy, Penna.
1891.	ZIEGLER, WALTER MACON LOWRIE, M. D.,	Philadelphia.

TOTAL MEMBERSHIP, JULY 4, 1892, 546.

Necrological Roll.

DIED.		RESIDENCE.
1891.	BIDDLE, ALGERNON SYDNEY, . .	Philadelphia.
1891.	DAVIS, EDWARD MORRIS, Jr., . .	Philadelphia.
1892.	DORRANCE, CHARLES, ...	Wilkes-Barre, Penna.
1890.	FOX, DANIEL MILLER, ...	Philadelphia.
1892.	JACKSON, LEWIS BUSH, ...	Philadelphia.
1892.	JAMES, CLARENCE GRAY, ...	Philadelphia.
1891.	LEIDY, PHILIP, M. D., ...	Philadelphia.
1891.	LOCKWOOD, ELON DUNBAR, . . .	Philadelphia.
1892.	MARSHALL, FRANCIS RIDGWAY, .	Philadelphia.
1891.	PAULSON, CHARLES HENRY, Jr., . .	Pittsburgh, Penna.
1892.	PHELPS, JOHN CASE, ...	Wilkes-Barre, Penna.
1892.	STICHTER, THOMAS DIEHL, ...	Reading, Penna.
1892.	WATKINS, SAMUEL POTE, Jr., . . .	Philadelphia.

www.ingramcontent.com/pod-product-compliance
Lightning Source LLC
Chambersburg PA
CBHW021604270326
41931CB00009B/1359